MORNING MEDICINE

Empowering Prayer Practices for Resilience
in Modern Challenges: A 52-Week Journey of Speaking,
Interceding, Listening, Trusting, and Responding
to the Spirit of God Through Adversity and Beyond

BISHOP BYRON L. SMITH SR., M.DIV., MA, D.D.

Morning Medicine: Empowering Prayer Practices for Resilience in Modern Challenges

For information contact: Byron L. Smith Sr., (https://www.lifting3veils.com/)

Book Publishing Consultant: Cedric Nesbitt (https://www.cedricdnesbitt.com/)

Editor & Publishing Consultant: Sinyon Ducksworth (letthepaperspeak.com)

ISBN: 979-8-9904350-0-1 (paperback)

1st edition

Contents

Acknowledgements

Special appreciation for my lovely wife of 33 years, Jill, our children ByRon II, AaRon, DeRon, Imani; My mother Patricia Walker, my grandchildren and siblings.

Special gratitude to: Bishop Dotcy I. Isom & Mrs. Isom, Bishop & Mrs. Henery M. Williamson, Mrs. Phedondia Johnson (One Church One School), Elder Carrell K. Cargle Sr., Bishop Paul A. G. Steward & Mrs. Steward, Bishop Sylvester Williams & Mrs. Williams, Bishop James A. Ross & Mrs. Ross (United Christian Communion), Rev. Mrs. Roland Brown, Dr. Kristian DeTroyer (Claremont School of Theology Professor), Dr. Roland Farber, and Dr. Lincoln Galloway (Claremont School of Theology Professor).

Dedication

For my children, grandchildren, family and friends,

May you start each and every week that you are granted by God, to remain intentional about spending some influential time with Him before your work week gets clouded or filled up with business and noise.

Connect and be led by the Spirit of God.

Seek to understand what God intends for you each week, rather than letting ego tell the week what you are planning to do with it.

From the Bishop's Desk

Two days that are certain and set in stone: the day that we are born into the world and the date that God has set aside for us to depart from this world. Everything between those two dates, God has given us a fair opportunity to draw closer to him. We should become good stewards of the time we've been given.

When God placed the concept of daily prayer and devotional moments in my heart, it was with a profound sense of purpose. This sacred time, set aside first thing in the morning, serves as a cornerstone for the day ahead. It's an invitation to align my mind, heart, body, and soul with the Divine, creating a harmonious start that resonates through every moment that follows.

This practice is not merely a ritual but a deliberate act of tuning into God's frequency before the world sets in with its demands, distractions, and noise. It's about acknowledging the presence of the Divine within and around us, fostering a spiritual connection that guides our thoughts, actions, and decisions throughout the day. This moment of communion is a reminder that we are not alone in our journey. God walks with us, offering wisdom, strength, and comfort.

The morning prayer and devotion is an acknowledgment of our dependence on God's grace. It's a time to express gratitude for the new day, for life, health, and opportunities. It's a space to bring our worries, hopes, and dreams before God, laying them down at His feet with trust and faith. This act of surrender allows us to start the day with a lighter heart, free from burdens that we are not meant to carry alone.

Moreover, this daily practice sharpens our spiritual senses, making us more attuned to God's voice and guidance. It's a process of opening our hearts to receive divine wisdom, which illuminates our path and helps us discern the steps we are to take. It cultivates a deep sense of peace and confidence, knowing that we are aligned with God's will, which is perfect and pleasing.

In essence, the concept of "Morning Medicine" daily prayer and devotional moments is about creating a sacred space for God at the very beginning of our day. It's an acknowledgment of His sovereignty and a testament to our faith. This spiritual discipline shapes, molds, and transforms us, enabling us to live out our purpose and calling. It's a journey of becoming more like Christ, as we reflect His love and light in a world that desperately needs it.

As we commit to this daily practice, we find that it's not just our mornings that are transformed but our entire lives. We become more patient, loving, and compassionate. We navigate life's challenges with grace and resilience. We become beacons of hope and faith, impacting those around us in profound ways. This daily moment of prayer and devotion is not just for our benefit but serves as a channel through which God's love flows into the world.

Starting each day with prayer and devotion is a divine strategy for living a life rich in faith and aligned with God's will. It prepares us spiritually, emotionally, and mentally to face whatever the day may bring, with the assurance that God is with us every step of the way. This sacred time sets the tone for a day lived in close communion with the Divine, a day where we can truly say, "Not my will, but Yours, O God, be done."

Sincerely,

Bishop Byron L. Smith Sr.

Lifting The Veil, Inc., Los Angeles, CA.
www.lifting3veils.com

Presiding Bishop at:
Gethsemane Christian Love MBC, Los Angeles, CA.

Why Devotional Prayer?

Why should you embark on this journey of devotional prayer?

Connecting with God through prayer is a profound practice that can enrich your life in countless ways. Applying scripture enriches the understanding of the power and importance of prayer and scripture. Here are some compelling reasons to start and maintain a powerful connection with God through prayer:

1. Inner Peace - Prayer offers a peace that is deep and enduring, inviting God's tranquility into our lives.

> "Do not be anxious about anything, but in every situation, by prayer and petition, with thanksgiving, present your requests to God. And the peace of God, which transcends all understanding, will guard your hearts and your minds in Christ Jesus." - Philippians 4:6-7.

2. Guidance - In seeking divine guidance through prayer, we open ourselves to God's generous wisdom.

> "If any of you lacks wisdom, you should ask God, who gives generously to all without finding fault, and it will

be given to you." - James 1:5.

3. Strength - Prayer connects us to the source of all strength, empowering us to face life's challenges.

> "But those who hope in the Lord will renew their
> strength. They will soar on wings like eagles; they will run
> and not grow weary, they will walk and not be faint." -
> Isaiah 40:31.

4. Hope - Prayer nurtures hope, reminding us of God's promises and faithfulness.

> "May the God of hope fill you with all joy and peace as
> you trust in him, so that you may overflow with hope by
> the power of the Holy Spirit." - Romans 15:13.

5. Gratitude - Prayer cultivates a grateful heart, helping us recognize and appreciate God's work in our lives.

> "Give thanks in all circumstances; for this is God's will
> for you in Christ Jesus." - 1 Thessalonians 5:18.

6. Transformation - Through prayer, we invite God to transform us, aligning our hearts with His.

> "Do not conform to the pattern of this world, but be

transformed by the renewing of your mind. Then you will be able to test and approve what God's will is—his good, pleasing and perfect will." - Romans 12:2.

7. Healing - Prayer is a powerful channel for healing, comfort, and forgiveness.

"Is anyone among you sick? Let them call the elders of the church to pray over them and anoint them with oil in the name of the Lord." - James 5:14.

8. Community – Praying with others fosters a sense of belonging and reinforces our connection to the body of Christ.

"For where two or three gather in my name, there am I with them." - Matthew 18:20.

9. Spiritual Growth - Regular prayer is crucial for deepening our relationship with God and growing in faith.

"But grow in the grace and knowledge of our Lord and Savior Jesus Christ. To him be glory both now and forever! Amen." - 2 Peter 3:18.

Scriptures serve as foundational pillars for a prayerful life, reminding us of the power, purpose, and promise of prayer. As you continue to explore your prayer devotional guide, let these verses inspire and guide you in your journey of faith.

Daily Prayer

Morning Medicine

Pause—*Prepare your heart for prayer. Bring yourself into present awareness.*

———◆◆◆———

O Gracious eternal Lord and Savior,

The Father of Abraham, Isaac, and Jacob. Remind us as your people today O God; that this is the day you have made and that we should rejoice and be glad about it.

Keep our minds and hearts open to you today, O Lord. Block out any other thought or deed that is not of you. Help us see today as a day wasted when we do not learn something new about you and for you. Help us, O God, to be individuals not wasting any time today that is not productive, but lead us on our way to goodness and to you. Help us in our attempts to do our work better every day. Help us add something to our store of knowledge and spirituality every day. Assist us in understanding someone more deeply each day. Allow us, O God, on this day to learn more of self-mastery and self-control under your spiritual power and guidance. Give us this day to better rule our temper and our tongue. Give us this day to leave our faults farther behind and grow more closer in the likeness of you, O Lord.

Give us this day, so as this day comes to a close our work spiritually, physically, and mentally will draw us and others closer to you. Continue to give us the light, so our light can shine brightly just for you, as you bless us on this day and the days to come. We promise to bless you back by blessing your name and your people.

In the name of the Father, Son, and Holy Spirit. Amen.

Now reflect—*Use the next page to describe your spiritual awareness after prayer.*

Prayer Notes

Monday Prayer

Morning Medicine

Pause—*Prepare your heart for prayer. Bring yourself into present awareness.*

———◆○◆———

O Gracious God,

We thank you for keeping us with your love one more day. We thank you for last night's rest, which we laid aside our daily work and tasks to relax our bodies, to give way for you to refresh our minds, and strengthen our spirits.

We thank you for the opportunity to worship you and give you thanks yesterday with freedom and peace. We were able to lay aside our cares and our anxieties to concentrate our every thought on You and You alone. We thank you for the worship experience. We thank You for the fellowship we enjoyed within it; the teaching, preaching, smiles, genuine hugs, and love given to us; and for the encouragement and guidance for life from Your living spirit which we received.

Lord, we thank You so much for the reading of Your word, for the preaching of Your word, for the singing of praise, for the prayers of Your people, and for Your Grace and Mercy, You have given to our worship experience.

Now O Lord, give us this day that we may receive strength and Your guidance, so that we will be enabled to go out to walk and talk with love, hope, faith, joy, long-suffering, and patience with your people, displaying that we have had an encounter with you on yesterday in worship service and this morning in prayer.

As you bless us, I promise to be a blessing back to you, by blessing your people.

In Jesus' name, I pray. Amen.

Now reflect—*Use the next page to describe your spiritual awareness after prayer.*

Prayer Notes

_____
_____
_____
_____
_____
_____
_____
_____
_____
_____
_____
_____
_____
_____
_____
_____
_____
_____
_____
_____
_____
_____
_____
_____
_____
_____
_____
_____
_____

Prayer of Thanks

Morning Medicine

Pause—*Prepare your heart for prayer. Bring yourself into present awareness.*

D ear Gracious and loving God,

The God of Abraham, Isaac, and Jacob. I come to you this morning to thank you for your unconditional love and mighty acts. Thank you for your kiss of grace, touch of love, and power that has given me life this morning. Thank you, O God! I love you and adore you. Now God, continue to bless me in your own way.

Forgive me for any transgressions I might have committed by word, thought, or deed. Bless me that my heart might be made right to stay in tune with you this morning and in the days to come. Stretch out your arms, O Lord, this morning and guide me in the way that you need me to go. Protect me and my family from dangers seen as well as dangers unseen.

Continue to lift us up as your people on this morning, O loving God, that we might bring light into the dark corners of this world. Continue to lift us up, O mighty God, that someone might come to know you better. Lift us up during this day, O wonderful God, in such a way that those who seek to do and bring your people harm and confusion, can be redirected by the light you have given us today.

Lift us up on this day, O mighty God, that those who believe can bring those from unbelief into a greater awareness that you are the source of power, healing, love, wisdom, comfort, protection, and life. Lift up men and women of God on this morning. Families, marriages, children, and grandchildren, the bereaved, the sick, the homeless, those incarcerated, the lost, the least, and the left out.

Bind any spirit that is not of you, so that we can move out into the world today with freedom and assurance on this day to help make this world a better place. So that the people of this world may know that you are the most high God. The Alpha and the Omega, the beginning and end of all things.

As you bless me to decrease, strengthen me by your Spirit, O Lord of Host. To be guided by you and you alone. I promise to bless you back, by blessing your name and your people.

In Jesus' name, I pray. Amen.

Now reflect—*Use the next page to describe your spiritual awareness after prayer.*

Prayer Notes

_____
_____
_____
_____
_____
_____
_____
_____
_____
_____
_____
_____
_____
_____
_____
_____
_____
_____
_____
_____
_____
_____
_____
_____
_____
_____
_____
_____

Consistent Blessings

Morning Medicine

Pause—*Prepare your heart for prayer. Bring yourself into present awareness.*

O Gracious God,

We thank you for your Love, your Mercy, your goodness, and your consistency in our lives. Now God we come to you again this morning requesting for your continued consistency of blessings. Bless us on this day that your Spirit would be in our minds, to guide our thoughts towards the truth according to your word. Bless us with your Spirit that our hearts will be cleansed to the point that any and every unclean desire would flee. Bless us with your Spirit, O gracious God, that our lips would be preserved to speak for you and you alone.

Bless us with your Spirit on today, O God, that our eyes may find delight in looking for your darling Son, Jesus. Bless us with your Spirit that our hands may be faithful today and eager to do Your will. Bless us with your Spirit, O God, that your Spirit will take over our lives, that our lives on this day and this week, may be strong with Your power, wise with your Wisdom, and beautiful with Your Love. Bless us on this day that our lives can in return be a blessing to many.

In Jesus' name, I pray. Amen.

Now reflect—*Use the next page to describe your spiritual awareness after prayer.*

Prayer Notes

Prayer for Guidance

Morning Medicine

Pause—*Prepare your heart for prayer. Bring yourself into present awareness.*

───────◆◇◆───────

D ear Gracious eternal God,

Thank you for being so loving, kind and just. Thank you for keeping things together in the universe, on earth, as well as in heaven. Thank you for ordering my life to see another day and keeping me even when I could not keep myself.

Now, O Gracious eternal God, forgive me where it is needed and bless me with your finger of love.

Send me out into this day with your spirit of kindness that my light will shine brightly before men and women that they might see my good works and glorify you and you alone. Send me out, O God, on this day with power that I might touch someone the same way you have touched my life.

Send me out, O God, that someone might know and understand that you are the light of the world. Send me out today, O Lord, that I might share with others your comforting, healing, and sustaining power.

Send me out today into this world dear Heavenly Father that someone might hear from you through my actions. Send me out today that I might give hope, comfort, wisdom, and Godly support, just like you have given to me.

Rest your comforting spirit upon those who have lost loved ones today or walking through a season of grief. Bless us on this day, so that we will be grateful for every breath we take to bless your name and your people.

In Jesus' name, I pray. Amen.

Now reflect—*Use the next page to describe your spiritual awareness after prayer.*

Prayer Notes

Prayer for Peace

Morning Medicine

Pause—*Prepare your heart for prayer. Bring yourself into present awareness.*

—————◆○◆—————

Dear Heavenly Father,

O gracious God. We come before You today with hearts full of gratitude for Your unending love and grace. We lift up to You, prayers for those who are in need of patience, Lord. Grant your servants the strength to wait on Your timing and the wisdom to trust in Your perfect plan. In moments of frustration and anxiety, fix the minds and hearts of all those who have faith. Fix the hearts of your people, hearts all over the universe. May your peace, O God, Your peace that surpasses all understanding, help us see Your hand at work in every situation, and remain steadfast in faith and love.

May all those who seek You, find solace in Your presence and be reminded that Your ways are higher than our ways, and Your thoughts higher than our thoughts. Surround us with Your love and encouragement, and let us be a light to others through their example of patience and trust in You.

In Jesus' name, I pray. Amen.

Now reflect—*Use the next page to describe your spiritual awareness after prayer.*

Prayer Notes

Heal Our World

Moring Medicine

Pause—*Prepare your heart for prayer. Bring yourself into present awareness.*

---◆◇◆---

Dear Gracious and loving God,

Thank you, O God, for being Omnipresent, Omniscient, life-giving, the El Olam, and the Jehovah-Jireh of my life and the world.

Now O God, hear my request today. I am feeling overwhelmed as we live in unrestful and unpredictable times within many individual homes, communities, cities, rural areas, and countries. Lord, I believe you today, but help me in my unbelief. Inspire all people across, race, gender, sexuality, and ethnicity; that if Your people, O God, who are called by Your name, will humble themselves and pray and seek Your face, O God, and turn from our wicked ways, that You, gracious God, will hear from heaven and heal our land.

O God, remind us that you rain on the just and the unjust. Inspire your people, O God, to turn from looking at you as a situational God to an everyday God. Inspire your people today to seek you first every day, not just when they thirst for healing and deliverance.

O merciful God, I welcome your spirit in my life today to clean things out of my mind, body, and soul that would hinder me from saying yes to your will and yes to your way for my life. I welcome you not just into my heart, but asking you to touch the hearts of those in the hospitals, the schools, the prisons, the homeless shelters, the drug houses, the drug treatment centers, and every home, city, state, and country. So that at the end of the day, our minds and hearts will give you glory and honor.

As you bless me and keep me in perfect peace with my mind and heart stayed on you, O Lord of Host, I promise, to bless you back by blessing your name and people.

In Jesus' name, I come to pray. Amen.

Now reflect—*Use the next page to describe your spiritual awareness after prayer.*

Prayer Notes

_____
_____
_____
_____
_____
_____
_____
_____
_____
_____
_____
_____
_____
_____
_____
_____
_____
_____
_____
_____
_____
_____
_____
_____
_____

A Light in Dark Times

Morning Medicine

Pause—*Prepare your heart for prayer. Bring yourself into present awareness.*

———◆○◆———

D ear O mighty God,

I come to you this morning with a humble heart, seeking Your divine guidance and presence. Lord, I ask for insight to understand Your will and purpose for my life.

Open my mind, God, to Your wisdom, that I may discern Your will and your way in all situations. Illuminate my path and the path of the universe so that I may walk in Your light and not stumble in darkness.

Grant me the strength to face each day with courage and resilience. When challenges arise, help me to stand firm in my faith, knowing that You are my refuge and my fortress.

Empower me and the world, O God, to overcome obstacles with grace and perseverance, leaning on Your strength rather than our own.

Fill me, gracious Lord, with Your wisdom. Lord, that I may make decisions that honor You. Let Your Spirit guide my heart today, my thoughts and actions; so, I may act with integrity and love.

Give me, Merciful Father, your understanding to navigate life's complexities with clarity and purpose, always seeking to glorify Your name's approval.

I thank You for Your constant presence and unfailing love. As you bless me, I promise to bless you back, by blessing your name and your people.

In Jesus' name, I pray. Amen.

Now reflect—*Use the next page to describe your spiritual awareness after prayer.*

Prayer Notes

Divine Connection

Morning Medicine

Pause—*Prepare your heart for prayer. Bring yourself into present awareness.*

———◆○◆———

Heavenly Father,

I come before You, O Gracious God, with a heart yearning for a deeper connection with You and Your people. Lord, I desire to be in spiritual alignment with Your will, walking in harmony with Your plans and purposes for my life. Draw me closer to You, that I may hear Your voice clearly and follow Your guidance faithfully.

Help us, as your people, to align our hearts and minds with Your truth, shedding any thoughts or actions that lead us astray. Fill us with Your Holy Spirit, that we may be attuned to Your presence and sensitive to Your leading. Let Your love transform us, making us more like Christ each day.

I also pray for unity with my brothers and sisters in Christ. Strengthen the bonds of fellowship among us, so that we may support, encourage, and uplift one another. Teach us to love as You love, to serve as You serve, and to forgive as You forgive. May our relationships reflect Your grace and bring glory to Your name.

Guide my heart and mind so that they may both work together in harmony. Guide me to work in harmony with my brothers and sisters, using our diverse gifts in the Church to build up the body of Christ and advance Your kingdom. Let us be a light in the world, united in purpose and mission, showing the world the beauty of a life aligned with You.

In Jesus' name, I pray. Amen.

Now reflect—*Use the next page to describe your spiritual awareness after prayer.*

Prayer Notes

_____
_____
_____
_____
_____
_____
_____
_____
_____
_____
_____
_____
_____
_____
_____
_____
_____
_____
_____
_____
_____
_____
_____
_____
_____

Unity Prayer for Love

Morning Medicine

Pause—*Prepare your heart for prayer. Bring yourself into present awareness.*

H eavenly Father,

We come before You, asking for Your love to fill our hearts and overflow into our lives. Teach us to love as You love, unconditionally and selflessly. Help us to see others through Your eyes, with compassion and grace. Let Your love transform our relationships, bringing peace and unity.

In Jesus' name, we pray. Amen.

Now reflect—*Use the next page to describe your spiritual awareness after prayer.*

Prayer Notes

Prayer for Forgiveness

Morning Medicine

Pause—*Prepare your heart for prayer. Bring yourself into present awareness.*

———————◄O►———————

M erciful Father,

I ask for Your forgiveness for the times I have strayed from Your path. Cleanse my heart and renew my spirit. Help me to forgive those who have wronged me, just as You have forgiven me. Fill me with Your grace and mercy, that I may extend the same to others.

In Jesus' name, I pray. Amen.

Now reflect—*Use the next page to describe your spiritual awareness after prayer.*

———————◄O►———————

Prayer Notes

Prayer for the Oppressed

Morning Medicine

Pause—*Prepare your heart for prayer. Bring yourself into present awareness.*

———◆○◆———

Dear Gracious and loving God,

The God of Abraham, Isaac, and Jacob. Thank you for this day. Thank you for the breath of life. Thank you for your guidance and protection. Thank you, O God, for your understanding, patience, power, and your timeliness.

Now all mighty God. Continue to fall down upon us as your people today and bless us. Bless everyone today who has breath in their bodies. For we know according to your word, that you and you alone rain down on the just as well as the unjust. Therefore, most merciful God, bless those who are facing injustice and oppression today. Give the oppressed strength to endure and the faith to stand.

Bless those who have power and position in this world and remind them to use their position and power wisely to honor your name. Bless those who are seeking help and relief to be guided to those who will operate with (Agape) love and humility to assist them in their deficiency.

Bless us today, O mighty God, to never overlook the least, the lost, and the left out. Continue to show your patience, O God, with those who have not realized that it's you who give the power and it's you who can take it away.

Bless those who are sick, weak, and feeble to be touched by your healing power. Encourage those who are losing hope to remain focused by faith and not by sight. Bless and strengthen those who are going through the loss of a loved one. Keep your loving and strong hand upon them. Continue to protect those who are being used and abused, physically, emotionally, and spiritually.

Remain mild-tempered with those who are misusing their position and power to fuel their own ego. Help your people, O God, all over the universe to decrease in ourselves and increase in you. Let justice run down like water and righteousness like a mighty steam on today and the days to come. So, at the end of the day, everyone would know and believe that we serve a God who can do all things but fail. As you guide and provide for us, O God, throughout this day and the days to come; to "keep the dream alive."

I promise to bless you back, by blessing Your name and Your people.

In the name of the Father, Son, and Holy Spirit. Amen.

Now reflect—*Use the next page to describe your spiritual awareness after prayer.*

Prayer Notes

Prayer for Hurting People

Morning Medicine

Pause—*Prepare your heart for prayer. Bring yourself into present awareness.*

---◆◇◆---

Dear Gracious eternal God. The father of Abraham, Isaac, and Jacob,

I thank you for blessing us to see another day. Now God, search me, and if you find anything that will hinder me from following your will today, fix it or remove it from my life so that I might walk according to thy will.

Bless those who are ill and need healing. Bless those who are lying in the operating room. Bless those who are battling sadness and depression. Bless those who feel broken. Bless those today who are perplexed about making the right decisions. Comfort those who are hurting and dealing with pain. Guide those who are looking for a way out of trouble and the right direction.

Strengthen those who are found weak today and protect those who are vulnerable to emotional and physical abuse. Encamp your protection angels all around us, so as we move throughout this day we can glorify and magnify your name.

Thank you for the doors of opportunities you have given us and the joy and peace to enjoy them. Now God continue to guide and empower us with your love so that we can express your love to your people, as you bless us and keep us.

I promise to bless you back by blessing your name and people.

In Jesus' name, I pray. Amen.

Now reflect—*Use the next page to describe your spiritual awareness after prayer.*

Prayer Notes

A Clean Heart

Morning Medicine

Pause—*Prepare your heart for prayer. Bring yourself into present awareness.*

———————◄O►———————

D ear Gracious and Loving God,

Thank you for your creative abilities and power. Thank you, Lord, for your abilities to create out of formlessness, darkness, void, and your power to still move.

Now God, create in all of humanity including me, a clean heart and right spirit that we might do Your most perfect will. Forgive us all who have sinned in the past whether those sins were words, thoughts, or deeds, forgive us.

Continue to bless us by creating in our eyes a fresh look on life, a new melody to hear a new song in our ears. A new vibe to feel and receive a fresh anointing from you. Bless us and move upon us to create new doors and possibilities to open up for our lives.

Bless us and command old doors to shut, that no one can ever open again. Bless us on this day, O Lord, with your abilities to create and move to push storms past us, create circumstances and an atmosphere for us today that our enemies will become our footstool. Bless us on this day, O Lord, with your abilities to create and move that our footsteps would be ordered by you and our territories would be enlarged.

Move on this day that our talk, walk, and heart will be right everywhere we go. So that your name is known all over the face of the earth as being a name that is above every name, and that at your name every knee shall bow, and every tongue shall confess that you are Lord and Savior.

In Jesus' name, I pray. Amen.

Now reflect—*Use the next page to describe your spiritual awareness after prayer.*

Prayer Notes

_____
_____
_____
_____
_____
_____
_____
_____
_____
_____
_____
_____
_____
_____
_____
_____
_____
_____
_____
_____
_____
_____
_____
_____
_____
_____

Prayer of Grace

Morning Medicine

Pause—*Prepare your heart for prayer. Bring yourself into present awareness.*

---◆---

O Gracious God, our Lord and Savior,

Whose desire is for us to love and to serve one another, and who has created us for fellowship with you and our fellow brothers and sisters, give unto us all throughout this day the gifts and the graces we need to make us easy to live with.

Give us courtesy, that we may live every moment as if we were living at the court of the King. Give us tolerance, so that we may not be so quick to condemn what we do not like and what we do not understand. Give us, on this day, considerateness, that we may think of the feelings of others even more than of our own.

Give us, on this day, Gracious Lord, the kindliness that we may miss no opportunity to help, to cheer, to comfort, and to encourage others to know that you are Great. Give us honesty, that our work may be our best, whether there is one or one thousand to see it. Give unto us this day to live in such a way that the world may be a better place because we passed through it with your power strengthening us and your Grace giving us one more chance to do your will.

As you Bless me with your Love, Power, and Grace. I promise to Bless you back by Blessing your people.

In the name of Jesus Christ, I pray. Amen.

Now reflect—*Use the next page to describe your spiritual awareness after prayer.*

Prayer Notes

Prayer for Covering

Morning Medicine

Pause—*Prepare your heart for prayer. Bring yourself into present awareness.*

---◆○◆---

D ear Most Gracious God,

The Father of Abraham, Isaac, and Jacob, whose love is over every person, place, and thing whom your hands have made. Touch us today, O God, as we go out this morning to the world and our work, I ask you, O God, to bless us.

Bless all classes and conditions of men and women, boys and girls everywhere. Bless those who are servants and help us to serve with diligence, and bless those who are in leadership positions and help us to direct and control with justice and mercy.

Bless those who are rich and help them to remember that they must hold all their possessions in stewardship for You, O God. Bless those who are poor so that they may find others to bless them.

Bless those who are strong and fit, and grant that they may never use their good health selfishly; bless those who are weak and ailing and keep them from all discouragement and discontent.

Bless those who are happy and full of joy and help them not to forget you, O Lord, in the sunny weather; and bless those who are sad, and ease the pain, comfort the loneliness of their hearts. Bless each one of us, that we may go out to love as those who have had an encounter with you on this morning, O Lord.

As you bless us throughout this day, I promise to bless you back by blessing your name and your people.

In Jesus' name, I pray. Amen.

Now reflect—*Use the next page to describe your spiritual awareness after prayer.*

Prayer Notes

_____
_____
_____
_____
_____
_____
_____
_____
_____
_____
_____
_____
_____
_____
_____
_____
_____
_____
_____
_____
_____
_____

Empowerment Prayer

Morning Medicine

Pause—*Prepare your heart for prayer. Bring yourself into present awareness.*

D ear Gracious all-knowing God,

Thank you for this day and this moment to connect with you one more time in prayer. I am so grateful and thankful!

Now God, touch me on this day that I might be empowered by your spirit to make decisions which is going to affect my whole life. Help me to choose the right way. Guide me, and with it grant me the humble obedience to accept it.

Help me, on this day, not to choose what I want to do, but what you, all mighty God, would like for me to do. Help me that I may not be swayed too far off to the left or the right by fear or hope of gain, selfish love of ease or comfort, or personal ambition.

Help me on this day in humbleness and obedience to say unto you: "Lord what will you have for me to do?" Then give me the strength to make the right decision at the right time so that I might do the right thing for your name's sake and glory.

Bless me to be a blessing to your people. Amen.

Now reflect—*Use the next page to describe your spiritual awareness after prayer.*

Prayer Notes

_____
_____
_____
_____
_____
_____
_____
_____
_____
_____
_____
_____
_____
_____
_____
_____
_____
_____
_____
_____
_____
_____
_____
_____
_____
_____

Wisdom in New Seasons

Morning Medicine

Pause—*Prepare your heart for prayer. Bring yourself into present awareness.*

———————◆◇◆———————

Dear gracious eternal God,

The Father of Abraham, Isaac, and Jacob, the God who is the Alpha and Omega the beginning and the end. I thank you for who you are in my life and who I am in you.

Now, God, I come to you this morning asking for you to cover all Seniors (parents, grandparents, and great-grandparents). Cover their minds, bodies, and souls and keep them from danger and sickness.

Be with all of us as we attempt to develop a new normal in life and interact with the world, the people in the world, and you, O Lord.

Give us wisdom, insight, foresight, discernment, and peace to make the right decisions and moves at the right time to be blessed by only you, to be a blessing to many. Guard our minds that we will see the glass half full and not half empty.

Inspire our hearts to break all boundaries of fear, and doubt. Strengthen our bodies with your spirit to press through adversity, and stand in the midst of storms and heavy moments throughout this week.

Protect us from all things that might try to come against us from doing your most perfect well. Give us the faith to believe even when unbelief is all around us. So that during this day, our light will continue to shine brightly before men and women, boys and girls that your name will be glorified.

O God! Grant me the serenity to accept the things I cannot change, the courage to change the things I can, and the wisdom to know the difference. Living one day at a time; enjoying one moment at a time; accepting hardship as the pathway to peace; taking as He did, this sinful world as it is, not as I would have it.

Trusting that He will make all things right if I surrender to His will; that I may be reasonably happy in this life.

As you bless us and protect us, I promise to bless you back; by blessing your name and your people.

In Jesus' name, I pray. Amen.

Now reflect—*Use the next page to describe your spiritual awareness after prayer.*

Prayer Notes

_____
_____
_____
_____
_____
_____
_____
_____
_____
_____
_____
_____
_____
_____
_____
_____
_____
_____
_____
_____
_____
_____
_____
_____
_____
_____

Prayer for Men

Morning Medicine

Pause—*Prepare your heart for prayer. Bring yourself into present awareness.*

———◆◇◆———

D ear Gracious Almighty God,

I come to you this day believing that you can do all things but fail. I need you who is a faithful and loving God to lift up your mighty hand from heaven and rest it this morning upon our boys, young men, and men who are opening up their eyes to see another day.

O God, our Lord and Savior, help men this day to work faithfully while it's day because we know that night is coming where no man can work. Give our boys, young men, and men the strength that they may not put off until tomorrow's tasks which should be done today.

Give them peace of mind that they may not do grudgingly, that which should be done with a smile. Help men, O Gracious God, that they may never be content to render to anyone else that which is less than their best.

Help men all through this day to be strong, mindful, and wise to the tricks of the enemy.

Give men the motivation to always be honest, never to be guilty of any mean action or any sharp practice, and never to see an unfair advantage over others.

Help men, eternal God, throughout this day to work, study, fellowship, love, and be at peace with themselves in such a way that when the evening drops in the midst of the day, they can hear you say, well done, well done, well done!

Lord, we need your help today to do things well.

In Jesus' name, I pray. Amen.

Now reflect—*Use the next page to describe your spiritual awareness after prayer.*

Prayer Notes

Prayer for Leadership

Morning Medicine

Pause—*Prepare your heart for prayer. Bring yourself into present awareness.*

Dear Gracious eternal God,

We need you and you alone to continue to show your face, your power, your authority, your guidance, your protection, your grace, your mercy, and your love, towards us today.

O God, order our footsteps to be more like thee. Eternal everlasting God, lift us spiritually so that we will have life. Lift us O God emotionally that we will have peace within our hearts, and lift us up again, O God, that physically our behaviors will be pleasing in thy sight.

O God, work on the hearts and minds of the leaders in Washington D.C., every Governor, every Mayor, every Supervisor, every council person, and their families in such a way that they will be encouraged to protect and lead the same way you would lead and protect.

O God, encourage the hearts of your people to turn from their wicked ways to believe that you are capable to heal and to do all things but fail.

Bless those who have the faith to keep the faith, and those who are lacking in their faith to acquire the faith the size of a mustard seed; so, they too can move mountains and magnify your Holy name.

O Merciful God, activate common sense within your people to hear, follow, and trust in your voice and your voice alone. Block out all demonic forces that have blinded the hearts and minds of your people.

Bless the faith leaders of this world with enough faith to know that your Grace is sufficient and that your Mercy endures forever. So, that your people might believe and know the same.

Bless, Lord, that we will walk right, talk right, and be right so that the rest of the world might know that you are worthy to be praised.

Stop the madness, sickness, and deaths around Covid-19 and any other illnesses, Lord.

I promise to bless you back; by blessing your name and your people.

In Jesus' name, I pray. Amen.

Now reflect—*Use the next page to describe your spiritual awareness after prayer.*

Prayer Notes

Guide Our Steps

Morning Medicine

Pause—*Prepare your heart for prayer. Bring yourself into present awareness.*

D ear gracious and everlasting God,

Remind us before we do anything else or change our location, that without you we can't do anything, be nothing, or understand anything. But with you, all things are possible.

Now Lord our God, in whom we live and move and have our being, help us never to forget that you, and you alone are beside us throughout this day.

O gracious God, who promised that you will be with us always, help us to never forget who you are and who we are in you. Guide us all day long, and all week long, that every word we speak may be fit for you, O God, to hear; that every deed that will happen with the body in which you have made for us may be fit for you to see; that every thought of our mind and every emotion of our heart may be fit to bear your examination.

O God, give us the strength on today that every task we do may be so well done that we can take it and show it to you at the end of the day. Allow every pleasure in which we share may be so honest and clean that we can ask You to share it with us.

So, bring us to the evening time with nothing left undone, and nothing badly done; with nothing to regret and nothing to make us ashamed. Help us to be fit for this day and the days to come.

As you bless us throughout this day and the days to come, I promise to bless you back, by blessing your people.

In Jesus' name, I pray. Amen.

Now reflect—*Use the next page to describe your spiritual awareness after prayer.*

Prayer Notes

Hope and Salvation

Morning Medicine

Pause—*Prepare your heart for prayer. Bring yourself into present awareness.*

———◆◇◆———

Dear Gracious Almighty God,

Here we are again, kissed by another wonderful morning. I am so thankful that you and you alone were inspired enough to bless us with another opportunity to see one more day.

God, here I am again, to say thank you. It feels so good and even great, to know that you will take care of me today just like you did yesterday. Now God, grant my request to continue to remind me as you move me along this day, that you are my Light and Salvation.

Continue to remind us, that you are our Rose of Sharon, continue to remind us, that you are our Hope for the now and our hope for the future. Continue to remind us on every street we walk down, on every highway we move down, on every stair we climb, on every chair we sit in, every classroom we enter to learn, every room or building we enter to gain income, every hospital we enter and leave to see and hear about sickness being removed from your people, every store we enter and have the means to buy something.

Remind us at every opportunity that our mouths are open to speak, on every opportunity to take a breath in and to exhale, and at every precious moment that we have an encounter with You and Your people, O Heavenly Father.

Remind us that without you, things are impossible, but with you All Things Are Possible!

In Jesus' name, I pray. Amen.

Now reflect—*Use the next page to describe your spiritual awareness after prayer.*

Prayer Notes

_____
_____
_____
_____
_____
_____
_____
_____
_____
_____
_____
_____
_____
_____
_____
_____
_____
_____
_____
_____
_____
_____
_____
_____
_____
_____

Bless this Day

Morning Medicine

Pause—*Prepare your heart for prayer. Bring yourself into present awareness.*

Dear Gracious and precious eternal God,

Thank you, for being who you are to creation, the operation of this world, and to the process that will carry us from birth to eternal glory.

Now, God, we have come this far by faith. Understanding that we cannot do anything without you and your power.

Therefore, gracious God, touch this world and your people to work while it's day. Help and remind us to smile while it's day. Help and remind us to forgive those who need it while it's day.

Help us to empower people with the gifts you have given us, while it's day. Help and remind us to study and believe more in your inspired word, while it's day.

Help us to encourage one another with good fellowship, while it's day. Give us peace within our hearts to respect one another, while it's day.

Because we know that night will come when no man or woman can work. Therefore, Gracious God, help us to surpass the dark things of this day so that our light will continue to shine brightly.

Blessed this day so that I can be a blessing to others.

In Jesus' name, I pray. Amen.

Now reflect—*Use the next page to describe your spiritual awareness after prayer.*

Prayer Notes

_____
_____
_____
_____
_____
_____
_____
_____
_____
_____
_____
_____
_____
_____
_____
_____
_____
_____
_____
_____
_____
_____
_____
_____

Prayer for the Sick

Morning Medicine

Pause—*Prepare your heart for prayer. Bring yourself into present awareness.*

———◆○◆———

D ear Gracious and loving God,

The Father of Abraham, Isaac, and Jacob. The Father who created the Heavens and Earth. We come to you this morning to say thank you for your goodness, strength, and mercy. Thank you for your unwavering love and kindness.

Now Gracious God, look down upon us and release unto us your spirit. Your spirit, which can bring forth life, love, joy, peace, patience, kindness, goodness, faithfulness, gentleness, self-control, and healing. Release your spirit and power to heal those who are suffering from and going through treatment for cancer, depression, high blood pressure, anxiety, Multiple Sclerosis, and Diabetes.

Bless those, O healing God, who are going through times of memory loss due to Alzheimer's and dementia. Bless those, O loving God, who are struggling with having strokes and any other type of illnesses and physical setbacks.

Continue to bless all doctors and nurses, O merciful Lord, that they may be in a position to be a blessing to your people. Give strength, sympathy, and empathy to the family members who are left in charge at home and convalescent homes to handle loved ones who are dealing with some sort of sickness.

Give those whom you have ordained to be caregivers the patience, understanding, and love to do the job and to do the job well. And for those who have not been ordained to care for the sick give them the right mindset and the humility to reach out to those whom you have called to get the job done so that your name will get all of the glory.

Give peace and hope to those who are going through the process and remind them not to be weary in well doing: for in due season, all reap, if we faint not.

As you bless the sick, the doctors and nurses, and the at-home care-givers, I promise to bless you back by blessing your name and your people.

In the name of the Son, Father, and the Holy Spirit. Amen.

Pause—*Prepare your heart for prayer. Bring yourself into present awareness.*

Prayer Notes

_____
_____
_____
_____
_____
_____
_____
_____
_____
_____
_____
_____
_____
_____
_____
_____
_____
_____
_____
_____
_____
_____
_____
_____
_____
_____

Prayer for Joy

Morning Medicine

Pause—*Prepare your heart for prayer. Bring yourself into present awareness.*

L oving Father,

I seek the joy that comes from knowing You.

Fill our hearts with Your divine joy, even in times of trial and hardship. Help us to find contentment and happiness in Your presence, and to spread that joy to those around us. Let Your joy be our strength.

In Jesus' name, I pray. Amen.

Now reflect—*Use the next page to describe your spiritual awareness after prayer.*

Prayer Notes

_____
_____
_____
_____
_____
_____
_____
_____
_____
_____
_____
_____
_____
_____
_____
_____
_____
_____
_____
_____
_____
_____
_____
_____
_____
_____
_____
_____

Love and Mercy

Morning Medicine

Pause—*Prepare your heart for prayer. Bring yourself into present awareness.*

O Gracious everlasting God,

We thank you today for your Love, your Mercy, your Power, your understanding, your Grace, and your Goodness.

O God, we understand that you are at all places at all times in the Universe. However, drop down into our hearts this morning. Fill us with your Spirit that we may move like you, talk like you, reason like you, stand strong like you, have faith like you, work like you, and shine like you.

Fill us today that our hearts and minds will take us where you would like for us to go and carry us, O Gracious God, today where you, and you alone, can open up doors for us that no one can shut and close doors that no one can open again. So that your will would be carried out today in our lives.

We need you, O Lord, to direct us with your Love, make us with your Mercy, pick us up with your Power, guide us with your Grace and Goodness, and lift us up with your everlasting Love. So that no matter what state the day may find us, we can share with the world your spirit of joy, hope, and happiness along with contentment wanting for nothing because of our encounter with you this morning.

O Gracious Lord, as you bless us, grant us our request, and enlarge our territory to be used by you and you alone.

I promise to be a blessing back to you by blessing your people.

In Jesus' name, I pray. Amen.

Now reflect—*Use the next page to describe your spiritual awareness after prayer.*

Prayer Notes

Prayer for Faith

Morning Medicine

Pause—*Prepare your heart for prayer. Bring yourself into present awareness.*

———◆○◆———

F aithful loving Father,

Strengthen our faith in You. Help us to trust in Your promises and rely on Your strength. When doubts arise, remind us of Your faithfulness and love. Guide us to walk by faith and not by sight, keeping our eyes fixed on You.

In Jesus' name, we pray. Amen.

Now reflect—*Use the next page to describe your spiritual awareness after prayer.*

———◆○◆———

Prayer Notes

Prayer for Gentleness

Morning Medicine

Pause—*Prepare your heart for prayer. Bring yourself into present awareness.*

———◦———

G racious and Merciful Father,

Cultivate within your people a spirit of gentleness. Help us to approach others with kindness and humility. Let our words and actions reflect Your gentleness and love. Teach us to be patient and understanding, bringing peace into every situation.

In Jesus' name, we pray. Amen.

Now reflect—*Use the next page to describe your spiritual awareness after prayer.*

———◦———

Prayer Notes

Prayer for a Second Chance

Morning Medicine

Pause—*Prepare your heart for prayer. Bring yourself into present awareness.*

———◆○◆———

R edeeming Father,

We thank You for being the God of second chances. When we fall short, lift us up and set us on the right path again. Help us to learn from our mistakes and grow in Your grace. Fill us with hope and determination to live according to Your will.

In Jesus' name, we pray. Amen.

Now reflect—*Use the next page to describe your spiritual awareness after prayer.*

———◆○◆———

Prayer Notes

Prayer for Comfort

Morning Medicine

Pause—*Prepare your heart for prayer. Bring yourself into present awareness.*

------◆◇◆------

Dear Gracious and loving God,

Thank you for allowing us to see another day. Thank you for your Grace and Mercy.

Almighty God, bless this day so we will walk with humility, faith, love, hope, kindness, and power. Remind us that we are your people and that you are our God. Blessed this day, O God, that the sick can be healed, the homeless will find shelter, and the lost will be found.

Bless this day, Eternal God, that protection will rest upon our schools. Bless this day, O God, that the minds and hearts of our young people in schools across the world, their footsteps will be ordered by your power.

Comfort those who are faced with the loss of a loved one. Strengthen the hearts and minds of the mature seasoned population so that they will make the right decisions at the right time to be an inspiration to those who are looking for positive and Godly direction.

Control and dissipate the spirit of divisiveness. Forgive those individuals who have looked the other way for personal gain when they had the position and means to make a difference. Lift and give strength to those who are afraid to take a stand for what is right.

Comfort those who are suffering because of wrong, which has gone forth, and give peace on this day to those who are willing to stand just for you, O God.

We need you, can't make it without you. Nevertheless, remind us throughout this day, that with you all things are possible.

As you guide and provide for us today, I promise to bless you back, by blessing your name and people.

In the name of the Father, Son, and Holy Spirit. Amen.

Now reflect—*Use the next page to describe your spiritual awareness after prayer.*

Prayer Notes

Led by the Spirit

Morning Medicine

Pause—*Prepare your heart for prayer. Bring yourself into present awareness.*

———————————◆○◆———————————

O Gracious God,

We thank you for your Love, your Mercy, your goodness, and your consistency in our lives.

Now, God, we come to you again this morning requesting for your continued consistency of blessings. Bless us upon this day that your Spirit would be in our minds, to guide our thoughts towards the truth according to your word. Bless us with your Spirit that our hearts will be cleansed so that any and every unclean desire will flee.

Bless us with your Spirit, O gracious God, that our lips would be preserved to speak for you and you alone. Bless us with your Spirit on today, O God, that our eyes may find delight in looking for your darling Son, Jesus. Bless us with your Spirit that our hands may be faithful today and eager to do Your will.

Bless us with your Spirit, O God, that your Spirit will take over our lives, that our lives on this day and this week, may be strong with Your power, wise with your Wisdom, and beautiful with Your Love. Bless us on this day that our lives can in return be a blessing to many.

In Jesus' name, I pray. Amen.

Now reflect—*Use the next page to describe your spiritual awareness after prayer.*

Prayer Notes

A Shining Light

Morning Medicine

Pause—*Prepare your heart for prayer. Bring yourself into present awareness.*

Dear Gracious eternal God,

Thank you for being so loving, kind and just. Thank you for keeping things together in the universe, on earth, as well as in heaven. Thank you for ordering our lives to see another day and keeping us even when we could not keep ourselves.

Now, O Gracious eternal God, forgive us where it is needed and bless us with your finger of love. Send us out into this day with your spirit of kindness that our lights will shine brightly before men and women that they might see our good works and glorify you and you alone.

Send us out, O God, on this day with power that we might touch someone the same way you have touched our lives. Send us out, O God, that someone might know and understand that you are the light of the world. Send us out today, O Lord, that we might share with others about your healing and sustaining power.

Send us out today into this world, dear Heavenly Father, that someone might hear from you through us. Send us out today that we might give hope, comfort wisdom, and Godly support, just like you have given to us.

Bless us on this day, so that we can be a blessing to your people.

In Jesus' name, I pray. Amen.

Now reflect—*Use the next page to describe your spiritual awareness after prayer.*

Prayer Notes

New Mercies

Morning Medicine

Pause—*Prepare your heart for prayer. Bring yourself into present awareness.*

---◆○◆---

Dear Gracious almighty God,

The maker of Heaven and Earth. The great I AM. The awesome ruler. The way maker, the healer, the guider and provider.

I come to you this morning to say thank you for being who you are in our lives. I come to thank you for being so wonderful in unpleasant situations in our lives as our protector. We thank you, O Lord, for keeping us from danger; healing us from sickness, stabilizing us in chaos, and lifting us up over our trouble. I come, to say thank you.

Now, O gracious God, continue to look down upon us today and continue to touch us with new mercies. Touch us in such a way that something will take over from within us that your new mercies will be recognized by us all day long. That our hearts might be transformed and inspired to walk better, talk better, and do better towards you and your people.

Help us not to get distracted or influenced today and throughout this week by individuals or groups who appear to walk in Holiness, but have ulterior motives to kill, steal, and destroy the path of righteousness.

Give us a greater sense of discernment today to identify your Will for us, over every other motive throughout every person, place, or thing that we may encounter today. Assist us not to judge nor look down upon anyone, but to guide us to stay on track with humility so that you may guide us towards peace, love, hope, patience, kindness, faithfulness, and happiness.

O God, touch our youth and young adults of today, touch the sick and afflicted, touch the broken heart, touch those today who are mentally unstable, preying on your young girls and boys in human trafficking, touch those who are battling with depression and anxiety and are incarcerated. O God Almighty, guard and protect our troops and their loved ones and bring them back home safe, sound, and sane.

We need you, O God, in the times we are living in, we clearly understand that we cannot make it without you, O Lord. So, bless us as you see fit.

As you bless us and guide us, I promise to bless you back by blessing your name and your people.

In Jesus' name, I pray. Amen.

Now reflect—*Use the next page to describe your spiritual awareness after prayer.*

Prayer Notes

_____
_____
_____
_____
_____
_____
_____
_____
_____
_____
_____
_____
_____
_____
_____
_____
_____
_____
_____
_____
_____
_____
_____
_____
_____
_____
_____
_____
_____

Bless Our Leaders

Morning Medicine

Pause—*Prepare your heart for prayer. Bring yourself into present awareness.*

------♦------

Dear gracious and loving God,

The God of Abraham, Isaac, and Jacob. Thank you for your countless blessings. Thank you for your guidance and protection. Thank you for your grace and mercy. Thank you, O God, and you alone for your faithfulness in our lives.

Now, O most loving and gracious God, continue to order our footsteps according to your word.

Continue, O God, to bless this day with us (your people) in mind.

Bless our country and the leaders around the world who have been placed in a position to lead.

Bless our Churches, Temples, Synagogues, and Mosque, O God. Bless every city and their leaders.

Bless every school; public, private, and charter, and their leaders. Bless every hospital and their leaders. Bless every home and their leaders.

Bless every correctional facility and their leaders. Bless every homeless shelter and their leaders.

So that the world might know that without you we can do nothing, be nothing, nor understand nothing. But with you, we can do all things.

Grant the leaders within our nation and around the world the wisdom to understand better to do better.

Grant the religious institutions to be blessed with a Divine connection from you, so that they might inspire the believer/worshipper to have a Divine encounter and connection with you.

Remind the leaders who are leading our schools to pray before school starts and keep the prayer within their hearts.

Bless the medical professionals with healing power so that healing will continue to take place through every doctor's visit and surgery.

Bless every warden and their families and remind them to be a blessing to the inmates.

Bless every home so that they will train up a child in the way they should go for your sake and glory.

Bless the least, lost, and left out, that the world would be reminded of your word that the first shall be last and the last shall be first.

Bless this day, O God, that violence and murders in our communities and at our borders will cease.

Bless us, O God, the way we need to be blessed on this day and the days to come; so that everything that we do and say might be a blessing to someone else.

As you bless us and provide for us, I promise to bless you back by blessing Your name and Your people.

In Jesus' name, I pray. Amen.

Now reflect—*Use the next page to describe your spiritual awareness after prayer.*

Prayer Notes

Prayer for Repentance

Morning Medicine

Pause—*Prepare your heart for prayer. Bring yourself into present awareness.*

F orgiving Father,

We come before You with repentant hearts, seeking Your mercy and grace. We confess our sins and ask for Your forgiveness. Create in us a clean heart and renew a right spirit within us. Help us to turn away from sin and walk in Your righteousness.

In Jesus' name, we pray. Amen.

Now reflect—*Use the next page to describe your spiritual awareness after prayer.*

Prayer Notes

_____
_____
_____
_____
_____
_____
_____
_____
_____
_____
_____
_____
_____
_____
_____
_____
_____
_____
_____
_____
_____
_____
_____
_____
_____
_____

Guide Us in Truth
Morning Medicine

Pause—*Prepare your heart for prayer. Bring yourself into present awareness.*

Dear Gracious almighty God,

Thank you for giving us another golden opportunity to embrace a day we have never seen before. Thank you for being such a wise and loving God, of knowing just what we need and when we need it.

Now God, the Father of Abraham, Issac, and Jacob. Give us Your blessings today as we go out to meet this day. Give unto us the lips which speak the truth, but with every word, speak the truth in love, power, and a sound mind.

Give us the mindset to seek the truth; and grant that we may face the truth even when it hurts and condemns us, and that we may never shut our eyes to that which we do not desire to see. Give unto us the fortitude to stand for principle, but save us from stubbornness, and from magnifying things of no importance into principles.

Give us grace to conquer our temptations and to live according to thy will, but save us from the self-righteousness which will look down on anyone who may fall short. Give us the spirit to keep looking toward the hills, and the power to keep pressing our way toward the mark of the higher calling which is in Jesus, the Christ.

Throughout this day, gracious Lord, give us the strength and the gentleness not to be conformed to the ways of this world but be transformed by the renewing of our minds to be blessed, to be a blessing to your people.

As you bless us and keep us, I promise, to bless you back by blessing your people.

In Jesus' name, I pray. Amen.

Now reflect—*Use the next page to describe your spiritual awareness after prayer.*

Prayer Notes

Give Us Your Spirit

Morning Medicine

Pause—*Prepare your heart for prayer. Bring yourself into present awareness.*

Dear Gracious loving God,

We thank you for granting us the fresh air of this new day. We thank you for keeping us safe all night last night. We thank you for lifting us to rise with peace today.

Now, Gracious God, broaden our territory with your strength, power, and Mercy.

We need you to order our footsteps today in such a way that we will go where you need us to go and move how you need us to move.

Gracious God, allow us to overcome anything around us, in us, or over us, that might be contrary to your will for our lives on this day.

Inject us with a big smile, that frowns might flee, inject us with a great bill of joy, that sadness will move out of the way, inject us with hope, that doubt will not have room, inject us with a great portion of peace, that chaos will be removed, inject us today, O wonderful God, with your love, that an unloving spirit would feel uncomfortable.

Give us kindness so that we can be kind. Give us an injection of strength, and the understanding to handle and overcome anyone who may be a distraction or someone who might be sent to derail your most perfect will in our lives on today.

Forgive us where forgiveness is needed, guide us where guidance is needed, love us where love is needed, that we might be found complete throughout this day wanting for nothing.

Help us, so we do not dwell in the spirit of compromise, so that we may act on the things we need to act upon, so that we can be better today than we were yesterday.

Keep us even when we are at the point of throwing in the towel today when we cannot keep ourselves.

Give us Your spirit, so if You lead us into the hospitals today, your people will know that You are a healer.

If You lead us to those who are in captivity, your people will know that You can give freedom.

If You lead us to the brokenhearted, they too will now know that You can mend broken hearts, and if You so lead us into a storm, You can make peace be still, that the world might know You are a peacemaker.

Help us today, O Gracious Lord, so that no matter what state we might find ourselves in throughout this day we can be content because of our encounter with You this morning.

As you bless us on this day, I promise to bless you back by blessing your name and people.

In The name of the Father, Son, and Holy Spirit. Amen.

Now reflect—*Use the next page to describe your spiritual awareness after prayer.*

Prayer Notes

_____
_____
_____
_____
_____
_____
_____
_____
_____
_____
_____
_____
_____
_____
_____
_____
_____
_____
_____
_____
_____
_____
_____
_____
_____

Prayer for Help

Morning Medicine

Pause—*Prepare your heart for prayer. Bring yourself into present awareness.*

———◆———

Dear Gracious and loving God,

Thank you once again for blessing another day. Thank you for keeping the universe and the things that you have created and placed in the universe, in the palm of your hands. Thank you, most merciful, all-knowing God.

Now God, the Father of Abraham, Isaac, and Jacob. Continue to help us line up with your will on this day. Check our hearts, our minds, and our souls on this morning and if you find anything that requires adjusting, please do so that we might move throughout this day honoring your name above every other name.

Thank you for being such a faithful God in our lives that when the prayers go up, the blessings will and have, come down. Thank you, Lord, for being an understanding God in the hospitals, schools, shelters, jails, drug houses, and various homes.

Lord, continue to heal, comfort, and stabilize those who are in need, and stabilize those who don't even know that they are in need.

Help us to try to do our work better every day. Help us to try to add something to our store of knowledge every day. Help us to try to know someone better every day. Help us to forgive better, help us to Love one another better.

Give us the ability to learn more about self-mastery and self-control. Help us each day to rule or temper, our tongues under the power of the Holy Spirit. Help us each day to leave our faults farther behind and to grow more like you every hour and day.

Give us this day and the opportunity to spread the good news to someone who may be open to receiving; that you are a faithful God, a kind God, a just God, a powerful God, a merciful God, a loving God, a second chance God, a protecting God and an on-time God.

Bless this day for us that at the end of this day, we can bless you back by continually blessing your people.

In Jesus' name, I pray. Amen.

Now reflect—*Use the next page to describe your spiritual awareness after prayer.*

Prayer Notes

Your Holy Place

Morning Medicine

Pause—*Prepare your heart for prayer. Bring yourself into present awareness.*

———◆———

Dear Gracious O mighty God,

The God of Abraham, Isaac, and Jacob. I come to you today the only way I know how. That is with a bowed down head and a humble heart. Thank you for giving me a good night's rest and grace to see another day.

Now, O God, look down upon this universe and the people that dwell within, and if you find anything, O lord, that does not line up with your will and your way, I pray that you will render forgiveness.

O God, bless the hearts of your people around the world and speak to the hearts and consciousness of your people. Helping individuals who have breath not to take for granted life and the purpose for living for you.

Reach out to the spiritual body of believers and people who have lost loved ones to tragic gun violence and mass shootings. Bless them, O God, with comfort, strength, and peace. Continue to bless and protect all spiritual gatherings around the world so that no one would feel uncomfortable or afraid coming into a sacred space. A Holy place. So, that your people may have a spiritual encounter with you.

We need you, O God, to continue to touch, guide, and provide for us and lead us to do your most perfect will. Give us the strength today not to focus on the minor things of life and lose focus on the major things of living for you. So, at the end of the day, your name will still be classified as Holy in our lives and society.

As you bless us to be all that we can be on today and the days to come for your sake and glory, I promise, to bless you back by blessing your name and your people.

In the name of the Father, Son, and Holy Spirit. Amen.

Now reflect—*Use the next page to describe your spiritual awareness after prayer.*

Prayer Notes

A Forgiving Heart

Morning Medicine

Pause—*Prepare your heart for prayer. Bring yourself into present awareness.*

———◄○►———

Dear Gracious eternal God,

Thank you for blessing us, one more time, to be a part of another wonderful day.

Now, O precious God, help us all throughout this day to follow your Will, and do unto others, all that we would like to be done unto us.

Bless us with the ability to help others, as we would wish them to help us. Help us to forgive others as we would like for them to forgive us when we make mistakes.

Bless us to make the same allowances for others as we would wish them to make for us. Help us to have the same sympathy and empathy for others as we would wish them to have for us when we are going through the storms of life.

Bless us to have the same respect and tolerance for their views and the beliefs of others as we would wish them to have for our own. Bless us to try to understand others as we would wish to be understood.

Bless us, O God, in such a way that when we are in the presence of others in fellowship on the job, school, home, and community, we may see things with their eyes, think things with their minds, and feel things with their hearts.

So, we may be as kind to others as you have been unto us by sending us your only Begotten Son who suffered, died, and rose again to set us free.

As you bless us and keep us throughout this day, I promise to bless you back by blessing your name and people.

In Jesus' name, I pray. Amen.

Now reflect—*Use the next page to describe your spiritual awareness after prayer.*

Prayer Notes

Prayer for Healing

Morning Medicine

Pause—*Prepare your heart for prayer. Bring yourself into present awareness.*

———◆○◆———

H ealing Father,

We come to You in need of Your healing touch. Whether in body, mind, or spirit, bring Your restorative power to our lives. Comfort those who are suffering and bring relief to their pain. Let Your healing presence renew and strengthen us.

In Jesus' name, we pray. Amen.

Now reflect—*Use the next page to describe your spiritual awareness after prayer.*

———◆○◆———

Prayer Notes

Prayer for Remaining Focused

Morning Medicine

Pause—*Prepare your heart for prayer. Bring yourself into present awareness.*

———◆○◆———

G uiding Father,

Help me to remain focused on You and Your purposes for my life. Remove distractions that lead me away from Your path. Strengthen my resolve to pursue Your will with diligence and passion. Keep my eyes fixed on your Son, Jesus, the author and perfecter of my faith.

In Jesus' name, I pray. Amen.

Now reflect—*Use the next page to describe your spiritual awareness after prayer.*

———◆○◆———

Prayer Notes

Prayer for Understanding

Morning Medicine

Pause—*Prepare your heart for prayer. Bring yourself into present awareness.*

W ise Father,

Grant us understanding in all that we do. Open our minds to Your wisdom and insight. Help us to discern Your truth and apply it to our lives. Let Your understanding guide our decisions and actions, so that we may walk in Your ways.

In Jesus' name, we pray. Amen.

Now reflect—*Use the next page to describe your spiritual awareness after prayer.*

Prayer Notes

Our Great Helper

Morning Medicine

Pause—*Prepare your heart for prayer. Bring yourself into present awareness.*

———◆◇◆———

O Loving and Everlasting God,

Help us all through this day to live in such a way to bring help to others and joy to those who love us, and to you, O God.

Help us to be—Cheerful when things go wrong, Persevering when things are difficult, and Serene when things are irritating.

Enable us to be—Helpful to those in difficulties, Kind to those in need, and Sympathetic to those whose hearts are sore and troubled.

Grant us that—Nothing may make us lose our temper,

Nothing may take away our joy, Nothing may ruffle our peace,

Nothing may make us bitter towards anyone.

So that all through this day, all with whom we work, and all with whom we meet, may see in us the reflection of you, Lord.

We belong to you, and you are who we seek to serve.

In Jesus' name. Amen.

Now reflect—*Use the next page to describe your spiritual awareness after prayer.*

Prayer Notes

A Thankful Heart

Morning Medicine

Pause—*Prepare your heart for prayer. Bring yourself into present awareness.*

---◀O▶---

D ear Gracious eternal God,

How can I thank you for all of your bountiful blessings? When I look around and realize that I can see, I am inspired to say thank you!

When I take a moment to listen, and I realize that I have been blessed on this new day to be able to hear, my heart is fixed to say thank you.

When I realize how much you have poured your blessings on me and around me on this day, I just want to keep on saying, thank you!

Now everlasting God, touch us so that we might decrease in ourselves and increase in you. So that as you move us throughout this day, keep your hands on us, lifting us up over trouble, and covering and protecting us through danger seen and unseen. To keep our hearts, our minds, and our souls in the right position to say thank you for all of your mighty works.

So, when the end of this day comes, we will still be in the right position—spiritually, physically, and mentally to say thank you! As you bless us and keep us.

I promise to bless you back by blessing your name and your people.

In Jesus' name, I pray. Amen.

Now reflect—*Use the next page to describe your spiritual awareness after prayer.*

Prayer Notes

Let Our Light Shine

Morning Medicine

Pause—*Prepare your heart for prayer. Bring yourself into present awareness.*

O Gracious and Mighty God,

The Alpha and O Mega of our faith, who have given us to be lights in this dark world, help us throughout this day to be a help and an example to all whom we meet.

Help us, O God, to bring comfort to those in sorrow, and strength to those who are tempted.

Help us, Almighty God, to bring courage to those who are afraid, and guidance to those who do not know what to do.

Help us, Prince of Peace, to bring cheer to those who are discouraged, and encouragement to those who are depressed.

And fix this day, O God, so as we move among men, women, boys, and girls, let all whom we may encounter catch a glimpse in us of the Master, whose we are and whom we seek to serve.

This, I ask in the name of Jesus, the Christ, our Lord and Savior. Amen.

Now reflect—*Use the next page to describe your spiritual awareness after prayer.*

Prayer Notes

_____
_____
_____
_____
_____
_____
_____
_____
_____
_____
_____
_____
_____
_____
_____
_____
_____
_____
_____
_____
_____
_____
_____
_____
_____

Love Our Neighbors

Morning Medicine

Pause—*Prepare your heart for prayer. Bring yourself into present awareness.*

Dear Gracious Almighty God,

I come before you this morning believing and knowing that you are the King of kings and the Lord of lords. Blessed the Lord, O my soul: and all that is within me, bless his Holy name.

Bless us on this day that we will decrease in ourselves and increase in you. Forgive us and cleanse us, so throughout this day, we will be empowered to obey your most perfect Will and your Way.

Shape us and make us into what you need us to be. So that we can help and inspire others as we would like for others to help and inspire us.

Give us the strength to forgive others as we would wish them to forgive us when we fall short. Give us the power to press our way past and beyond those who wish ill will for our lives and our journey.

Give us peace and insight to have empathy and sympathy for those who we come into contact with and those who are wrestling with conflictual ideas and thoughts.

Help us, Lord, to receive your healing, peace, love, kindness, and wisdom. So, we may enter into others' spaces in such a way that we may see things with their eyes, think things with their minds, and feel things with their hearts.

Give us this day that we may be as kind to others as we would wish them to be to us. Give us the power to let our light shine for you and you alone.

This I ask, in Jesus' name. Amen.

Now reflect—*Use the next page to describe your spiritual awareness after prayer.*

Prayer Notes

Prayer for Patience

Morning Medicine

Pause—*Prepare your heart for prayer. Bring yourself into present awareness.*

O Gracious and Loving God,

Thank you for this day and thank you for this moment to connect with you one more time in prayer.

Now, most merciful God, touch us on this wonderful morning so that we might decrease in ourselves and increase to be more like you. Let the words of my mouth and the meditation of my heart be pleasing in thy sight.

O loving and great God, give unto us this day patience with things and patience with people. If there is anything that we might find difficult, give us the perseverance that we will not fall to defeat.

If we face any problems that are hard to solve, help us not to abandon them, until we have found the solution. If we make mistakes the first time, help us to try and to try again, until failure becomes success.

Help us all throughout this day to never lose our temper with people, no matter how unfair, unjust, annoying, and unpleasant they may become. Help us, O gracious God, to have time to listen to anyone who wants to talk to us about a worry, a problem, or a need.

Help us to be patient with those who are slow to learn and slow to understand. Help us all through this day to work as Jesus worked and to love as Jesus loved. So that at the end of the day, we can be called a disciple of yours by the way we loved one another.

As you bless us and help us throughout this day, I promise to bless you back by helping and being a blessing to your people.

In Jesus' name, I pray. Amen.

Now reflect—*Use the next page to describe your spiritual awareness after prayer.*

Prayer Notes

_____
_____
_____
_____
_____
_____
_____
_____
_____
_____
_____
_____
_____
_____
_____
_____
_____
_____
_____
_____
_____
_____
_____
_____

Our Gracious Father

Morning Medicine

Pause—*Prepare your heart for prayer. Bring yourself into present awareness.*

———◆○◆———

Dear gracious and everlasting God,

The Lord of all things. The God of Abraham, Isaac, and Jacob. We do not know what will come our way today and what will happen to us today. Nevertheless, whatever comes to us, guard our minds, bodies, and souls. Guide, strengthen, comfort, and control us all day long.

If temptation comes to us, give us grace to overcome evil and to do right, in the name of Jesus. If we have to make important decisions, give us guidance to choose the right way, and refuse our own way.

If it will be difficult to witness for you, O gracious God, give us the courage never to be ashamed to show *whose* we are and *who* we are in you. If things go well with us, keep us from all pride and keep us from thinking that we made it on our own merit.

If we shall know sorrow, failure, disappointment, and loss, keep us from all despair. Help us, O mighty God, never to give in.

O Gracious Lord and Light of the world, Light of my soul, continue to be with us on this day. Whatever light may shine or shadow that may appear, we may forever more live, walk, and talk as children of the Most High God.

Forgive and correct the minds and hearts of the individuals and institutions who have sinned against You, O Lord. Protect and strengthen the victims through the healing process. Give power and strength to the leaders in position to make a difference so that they may be inspired to act and do justly.

Bless the families who are grieving over the loss of loved ones; strengthen them and comfort them.

As you bless us, guide us, and provide for us, I promise to bless you back, by blessing your name and your people.

In Jesus' name, I pray. Amen.

Now reflect—*Use the next page to describe your spiritual awareness after prayer.*

Prayer Notes

Sunday Prayer

Morning Medicine

Pause—*Prepare your heart for prayer. Bring yourself into present awareness.*

———————◆———————

O God, our Heavenly Father,

We thank you for this day and every day that brings us closer to you.

We give you special thanks for giving us all mothers. We thank You for Your inspired Word, to tell us of how you operate with your people.

We also, thank you, Lord, for setting before us the deeds and words of our Lord, Jesus the Christ, in the days of His life in the flesh.

We thank you for blessing your people with the gift to sing and play instruments so that we might enjoy the wonderful music produced and the memories which stir up in our hearts.

We thank you for the open doors of prayer which no man or woman can ever shut.

We thank You for this day, called to lay aside the things of the earth and enter into your presence with thanksgiving. We thank you for the preaching of Your word, to comfort our hearts, to enlighten our minds, and to inspire our souls.

We thank You and You alone for opening our minds and hearts today, so that we might do everything to give Your name Glory.

Give us what we need, that we might be found blessed on every occasion to bless You back, by blessing Your name and people.

In Jesus' name, I pray. Amen.

Now reflect—*Use the next page to describe your spiritual awareness after prayer.*

Prayer Notes

Psalm 103 Blessing

Morning Medicine

Pause—*Prepare your heart for prayer. Bring yourself into present awareness.*

———————◄O►———————

D ear Gracious and loving God,

The God of Abraham, Isaac, and Jacob. Thank you for your steadfast love towards us on this day. Thank you for granting us the opportunity to rise to see another day.

Now Gracious and loving God. You know what we need even before we ask. Nevertheless, bless the Lord, O my soul; and all that is within me, bless his Holy name!

Bless the Lord, O my soul, and forget not all His benefits: Who forgives all your iniquities, who heals all your diseases, who redeems your life from destruction, who crowns you with loving kindness and tender mercies, who satisfies your mouth with good things, so that your youth is renewed like the eagle's.

Bless the Lord, O my soul, and all that is within me, bless His Holy name.

As you bless us on this day, Gracious Lord, I promise to bless you back by blessing your name and your people.

In Jesus' name, I pray. Amen.

Now reflect—*Use the next page to describe your spiritual awareness after prayer.*

Prayer Notes

A Prayer for the Next Generation

Pause—*Prepare your heart for prayer. Bring yourself into present awareness.*

Dear gracious eternal and everlasting God,

Heavenly Father, I come before You with a heart full of gratitude and reverence for You, O God, alone. I acknowledge Your sovereignty, grace, and the boundless love You have shown for me and the Universe through Christ Jesus.

Lord, I desire that You bless my heart, and renew in me a clean heart, and a right spirit so that my life, O eternal God, reflects Your will and a testament to Your goodness. Grant me the wisdom and strength to live in a manner that pleases You, O God. May all of my actions, words, and thoughts be aligned with Your divine purpose. Help me to embody the love, compassion, and humility that Christ exemplified so that in everything I do, I may glorify Your name.

Father, let my life be a beacon of light, inspiring others to seek and serve You. May my faithfulness and dedication to Your teachings encourage those around me to pursue a deeper relationship with You. Empower me, O God, to be a steadfast witness of Your grace, leading others by my example to the path of righteousness for righteousness' sake.

I pray for the next generation, Lord. Pour Your Spirit upon them, guiding and nurturing their hearts to grow in faith and commitment to You. Use me and all those who desire to serve You as instruments to teach and inspire Your people, so they too may live lives that honor and glorify Your name.

In every trial and triumph, let me remain rooted in the spiritual discipline of Your sacred Words, knowing that through You, O God, we are strengthened and sustained. May our collective lives be a testament to Your glory, encouraging others to embrace Your love, truth, and goodness.

In Jesus' name, I pray. Amen.

Now reflect—*Use the next page to describe your spiritual awareness after prayer.*

Prayer Notes

Prayer Notes

Prayer Notes

About the author

Bishop Byron L. Smith Sr. has distinguished himself as a dedicated servant leader, beginning his ministry at age 29 with his inaugural sermon on March 16, 1996. With a profound love for Jesus Christ, his family—including a 33-year marriage, four children, and seven grandchildren—the Church, and its congregation, Bishop Smith embodies the essence of spiritual and community leadership.

His leadership revitalized Gethsemane Christian Love (GCL), guiding it from division to unity. Installed as Pastor on April 24, 2022, and elevated to Bishop in July 2022, he has instilled values of intentionality, inclusivity, and accountability, ensuring ministry is conducted with decency and order.

Beyond pastoral duties, Bishop Smith focuses on fostering transformative change through mental health advocacy, faith-based initiatives, policy development, and educational training.

He actively participates in community initiatives, including the Empowerment Congress, Safer Streets in Los Angeles, LA County Faith Collaborative, NAACP of Compton, and the Faith Collaborative on Homelessness. He has served as a National Faith Leader for Vulnerable Children and West Coast Director of One Church One School out of Chicago, IL, focusing on education, empowerment, and trauma-informed services.

With over 3,000 hours of clinical mental health experience, Bishop Smith is advancing towards his License as an Advanced Alcohol Drug Counselor (LAADC). He works as a Primary Clinical Therapist at an adult substance abuse residential program in Orange County, CA.

As a Mental Health Clinician and Adjunct Professor at Antioch University and Azusa Pacific University, he teaches master's level courses in psychology and pastoral care/church health. His contributions to mental health education, cultural sensitivity, community organizing, and advocacy have earned him recognition in Illinois and California for his activism and volunteerism.

Bishop Smith holds two Master's degrees in Counseling Psychology from Argosy University and a Master's of Divinity from Claremont School of Theology, along with a Doctor of Divinity from Saint James Convergence School of Ministry in Los Angeles, CA.

Bishop Byron L. Smith Sr. is committed to bridging gaps between diverse communities and initiating systemic changes. His work inspires and mobilizes stakeholders towards collaborative and impactful community development.

Bishop Smith is the founder of Lifting the Veil, Inc., Los Angeles, CA. Learn more at www.lifting3veils.com.

Made in the USA
Columbia, SC
21 August 2024

40892698R00093